Let Freedom Ring

Brigham Young
Pioneer and Prophet

by Cory Gideon Gunderson

Consultant
Richard L. Jensen
Research Associate Professor of Church History
Joseph Fielding Smith Institute for Latter-day Saint History
Brigham Young University
Provo, Utah

Bridgestone Books
an imprint of Capstone Press
Mankato, Minnesota

Bridgestone Books are published by Capstone Press
P.O. Box 669, 151 Good Counsel Drive, Mankato, Minnesota 56002
http://www.capstone-press.com

Printed in the United States of America

Library of Congress Cataloging-in-Publication Data
Gunderson, Cory Gideon.
     Brigham Young: Pioneer and Prophet/by Cory Gideon Gunderson.
          p. cm. — (Let Freedom Ring)
     Includes bibliographical references and index.
     Summary: Traces the life of Brigham Young, from his Vermont childhood to his rise as the leader of the Mormon Church.
     ISBN 0-7368-1346-2 (hardcover)
     1. Young, Brigham, 1801–1877—Juvenile literature. 2. Church of Jesus Christ of Latter-day Saints—Presidents—Biography—Juvenile literature. [1. Young, Brigham, 1801–1877. 2. Church of Jesus Christ of Latter-day Saints—Presidents. 3. Mormon Church—Presidents.] I. Title. II. Series.
     BX8695.Y7 .G86 2003
     289.3'092—dc21   2001007705

Editorial Credits
Charles Pederson, editor; Kia Adams, series designer; Erin Scott, SARIN Creative, illustrator; Jennifer Schonborn and Juliette Peters, book designers; Kelly Garvin, photo researcher; Karen Risch, product planning editor

Photo Credits
Lake County Museum/Corbis, cover (large); Corbis/Gianni Dagli Orti, 13, Lowell Georgia, 24, Scott T. Smith, 40 (top), James L. Amos, 40 (bottom), 43 (top); Stockbyte, cover (small), 4, 8, 12, 20, 26, 38; Hulton/Archive, 5, 27, 36–37; North Wind Picture Archives, 6–7, 14–15, 19 (left), 22, 25; Special Collections Department, J. Willard Marriott Library, University of Utah, 7, 28, 42; Special Collections, University of Vermont Library, 9; Bettmann/Corbis, 10, 35, 39; Stock Montage, Inc., 17, 21, 33 (left); PhotoSphere Images, 19 (right), 33 (right), 43 (bottom); courtesy, Colorado Historical Society, 41

1 2 3 4 5 6 07 06 05 04 03 02

Table of Contents

1 An Unlikely Leader   4

2 A Difficult Childhood   8

3 Struggling for Religious Freedom   12

4 Escape to the West   20

5 Establishing the Promised Land   26

6 Remembering a Leader   38

Features

Map: Deseret and Utah   31

Timeline   42

Glossary   44

For Further Reading   45

Places of Interest   46

Internet Sites   47

Index   48

Chapter One

An Unlikely Leader

Brigham Young was an unlikely leader. He grew up poor and powerless. He attended only 11 days of school in his lifetime. As a young man, he often pronounced words incorrectly and was not a good public speaker.

As the leader of a religious group called the Mormons, Brigham stirred deep feelings in many people. The followers of this Church of Jesus Christ of Latter-day Saints loved Brigham. Many non-Mormons hated him and feared his religion. They disapproved of the many wives he had. Many people believed that Brigham wanted a separate Mormon country apart from the United States. This belief caused many people to fear him.

Later in his life, Brigham Young became the leader of the Church of Jesus Christ of Latter-day Saints.

In the mid-1800s, Brigham led the Mormons from danger in Illinois to freedom and safety in Utah. He also organized a way for Mormons from other countries to reach Utah. In all, about 62,000 people took the Mormon Trail west to Utah. Thousands more traveled by railroad.

A group of Mormon families leaves Iowa for Salt Lake City. In this illustration, the pioneers are not using covered wagons. Instead, they are pulling covered handcarts.

In His Own Words

Brigham was concerned about his spiritual life. He once said, "I do not care what men say about me. I want my character to stand fair in the eyes of my Heavenly Father."

Most people agree that Brigham became a great leader. As the Mormon leader, he became a powerful public speaker. No one in U.S. history led more people farther or as successfully. Brigham helped develop more than 350 towns in the West. Today, even non-Mormons admire Brigham's skill in organizing the westward journey and Mormon settlements.

Chapter Two

A Difficult Childhood

On June 1, 1801, Brigham Young was born in Whitingham, Vermont. He was the ninth of 11 children born to John and Nabby Howe Young.

In 1804, John and Nabby moved their children to New York. They hoped to find better farmland than the rocky Vermont land they left. Brigham and his brothers helped John with the farm. They also worked for other farmers.

Brigham's large family was poor. To earn money, the girls made and sold straw hats. In his spare time, Brigham fished and hunted to provide food for his family. Brigham's parents could not afford to send any of their children to school. Nabby educated Brigham at home.

In June 1815, Nabby died of tuberculosis. She had been sick with this lung disease since Brigham was born. She died shortly after his 14th birthday. Brigham and his sisters took over Nabby's household jobs.

Brigham was born in Whitingham, Vermont. In the 1800s, the town looked similar to the way it does in the photograph above.

Nabby's death was hard for the entire Young family. John had to care for his children by himself. Nabby had been a gentle, loving mother, but John disciplined his children with harsh words and physical punishment. He seldom smiled.

Brigham left home as a young man. He worked at many jobs for 10 years.

Brigham's Parents

Years after Nabby's death, Brigham shared his feelings about her: "Oh my mother—she that bore me [gave birth to me]—I can say no better woman ever lived in the world." Hard work and his father's discipline wore Brigham down. He said: "I was troubled with . . . feeling cast down, gloomy . . . I felt lonesome and bad."

Sent into the World

In 1816, Brigham's father married Hannah Dennis Brown. Her husband had died, and she was raising her children by herself. Together, she and John cared for their children.

In 1817, John told Brigham to leave the house and earn his own money. At the time, Brigham was 16 years old. During the next 10 years, he held several jobs. He built canal boats and worked at a pail factory. Brigham also made leather from animal skins. He repaired furniture, built cabinets, and painted houses. He became known as a skilled and honest worker.

Chapter Three

Struggling for Religious Freedom

In his early 20s, Brigham fell in love with Miriam Angeline Works. On October 5, 1824, the two were married. They joined the Methodist church.

Brigham and Miriam had an eventful marriage. They lived for four years in Bucksville, New York. In 1825, their first daughter, Elizabeth, was born there. In 1828, the family moved to Mendon, New York. In 1830, the Youngs' second daughter, Vilate, was born. Brigham ran his own carpentry shop until Miriam developed tuberculosis. As her illness worsened, Brigham spent less time in the shop and more time caring for his family. On September 8, 1832, Miriam died.

Searching for Answers

During Miriam's illness, Brigham had begun to learn about different religious beliefs. His parents had raised him as a Methodist. Yet he wanted more. Brigham

An 1846 drawing shows boys learning to be carpenters. In the 1830s, Brigham opened his own carpentry shop to earn a living.

happened to read the *Book of Mormon*. This book contains the holy writings of the Church of Jesus Christ of Latter-day Saints, called Mormons. The Mormon faith appealed to Brigham, and on April 14, 1832, he was baptized as a Mormon.

In October 1832, Brigham met Joseph Smith for the first time. Smith had founded the Mormon religion on April 6, 1830. Brigham was sure that Smith was a prophet, someone who claims to be a messenger of God.

Brigham's Faithfulness

Brigham became a faithful follower of Joseph Smith and the Mormons. In 1833, Brigham moved to

After he was baptized, Brigham began to preach at Mormon meetings.

The Second Great Awakening

In the early 1800s, many U.S. citizens searched for religious truth. This search was called the Second Great Awakening. People wanted the freedom to worship God in their own way. Many religions such as Mormonism encouraged people to follow the Bible closely.

Kirtland, Ohio. There he helped build the Kirtland Temple as well as homes for new church members. He began to preach a week after he became a baptized Mormon.

In Kirtland, Brigham met and fell in love with Mary Ann Angell. On February 18, 1834, Brigham and Mary Ann were married.

In February 1835, Smith organized the Council of Twelve Apostles. Brigham was one of the council's members. Like Jesus' 12 apostles in the Bible, Brigham and these apostles were supposed to convince people to join their religion.

The *Book of Mormon*

As a young man, Joseph Smith claimed he spoke to an angel named Moroni. He said that Moroni told him about the history of an ancient North American civilization. This history was written on golden plates. In 1830, Smith published this history as the *Book of Mormon.* Mormon beliefs followed Bible teachings, the *Book of Mormon,* and Smith's teachings.

In late 1837, Brigham helped move the Kirtland Mormons to Far West, Missouri. Smith had started a bank in Kirtland, but it failed. People who lost money blamed Smith and threatened his followers. The Kirtland Mormons joined the Mormons who already lived in Missouri. The total number of Mormons in Kirtland was about 2,000.

Religious Hatred

The Mormons were not safe in Missouri. People who were not Mormons were angry with the way Mormons banded together and voted alike in local elections. Some non-Mormons attacked the Mormons, who defended themselves.

On October 27, 1838, the Missouri governor declared that Mormons were the enemy. He added that Mormons must move from Missouri or be killed. Smith went to jail in exchange for his followers' safety. He asked Brigham and another apostle named Heber Kimball to take over the church in his absence.

The Mormons hoped for a safe home away from Missouri. As temporary church leader, Brigham helped about 8,000 Mormons move to Commerce, Illinois. They renamed the city "Nauvoo," from a Hebrew-language word that means "beautiful." In the spring of 1839, Smith escaped from jail in Missouri and rejoined his followers at Nauvoo.

The Mormons named Nauvoo after a word that means "beautiful."

In September 1839, Brigham left Nauvoo. He planned to sail for England and convince English people to join the Mormon religion. In March 1840, he sailed for England. During his time there, he convinced many people to become Mormons.

Return to Nauvoo

When Brigham returned to Nauvoo in 1841, he learned that Smith had announced new Mormon beliefs. One of the new beliefs was that God wanted Mormon men to marry and live with several wives at the same time.

The practice of one man being married to several wives at the same time is often called polygamy. Mormons instead used the term "plural marriage." Non-Mormons already worried about an army the Mormons had created and their habit of voting together. Plural marriages further angered non-Mormons. In 1842, Brigham married Lucy Ann Decker while he was still married to Mary Ann.

In 1844, Joseph Smith and his brother, Hyrum, were arrested and jailed in Carthage,

Illinois. Smith had ordered his followers to destroy a Nauvoo newspaper. On June 27, a group of men broke into their jail cell and killed the brothers.

Without Smith, the Mormons had to choose new leadership. On August 8, they voted to let the Council of Twelve Apostles lead the Mormons. Brigham led the apostles and all the Mormons.

Joseph Smith founded the Mormon religion. In 1844, a group of non-Mormon men killed him and his brother, Hyrum.

Chapter Four

Escape to the West

Smith's death did not calm anti-Mormon feelings in Illinois. Angry groups set fire to 150 Mormon homes outside Nauvoo. Brigham decided to move his followers to a safer place.

Brigham and other Mormon leaders looked for possible settlements for the Mormons. They prayed, studied maps of the West, and talked with western explorers. Mormon leaders decided to create a new home in a desert area called the Great Basin. Here, they believed Mormons could avoid non-Mormons because no whites had settled the area. Under Brigham's guidance, the Mormons began to prepare for the difficult trek.

In February 1846, Brigham and a group of Mormons began their 1,300-mile (2,100-kilometer) journey from Nauvoo. By May, thousands of Mormons were on the move. The trail they created became known as the Mormon Trail. In June 1846, the Mormons camped at Council Bluffs in present-day Iowa.

In February 1846, the Mormons left Nauvoo because other Illinois residents had burned nearby Mormon homes.

U.S. Army Captain James Allen brought news to Brigham at Council Bluffs. The U.S. government had begun the Mexican War (1846–1848). The government offered to pay Mormon men to help fight the Mexican army in California.

Brigham accepted the arrangement and sent 500 men to California. When these volunteers received their pay, they sent part of it to their families. In all, they sent about $71,000. The money helped these people buy food and supplies for the trek west.

Winter Quarters

After the army volunteers left for California, it was too late for the rest of the Mormons to continue to the Great Basin before winter. They decided to stop at

The Mormons gathered for religious ceremonies at Winter Quarters.

Write a Journal

Mormon children had a busy life on the trail. They swam, climbed rocks, fished, and played games. They also had serious responsibilities. Some children helped steer their family's wagon. Others gathered dried buffalo manure to use as campfire fuel. Some children repaired clothes or cared for sick family members.

Pretend you are a child on the Mormon Trail. Write a paragraph to describe how you feel on the journey. What do you see, hear, and think? Tell about the happy and sad events that occur on the trail.

present-day Omaha, Nebraska, and wait until spring. They called their temporary home "Winter Quarters."

By December 1846, almost 4,000 Mormons lived at Winter Quarters. They built log cabins and dugout houses to help protect themselves from winter's harshness. But disease and poor diet killed about 600 Mormons.

On April 5, 1847, Brigham and a small exploring party left Winter Quarters to continue west. The explorers reached the Great Basin in 111 days.

Myth and Fact

Myth: All Mormons shared Brigham's excitement about living in Salt Lake City.

Fact: Not all Mormons were excited. Brigham's sister-in-law Harriet Decker Young saw the area for the first time. She said that she would rather walk another thousand miles than remain in that desert.

They walked and drove wagons from one water source to another. They crossed deserts, rivers, mountains, and prairies.

In July 1847, Brigham viewed the Mormons' new home for the first time. It was near a shallow lake called the Great Salt Lake. Brigham called the area "Deseret." This word comes from the *Book of Mormon* and means "honeybee." Like honeybees, the

The carved beehive at the top of this stair post is a symbol of Mormon hard work.

Mormons considered themselves helpful to each other and hard working. Brigham's exploring party quickly began to build houses inside a fort to protect themselves from American Indian attacks. They named their settlement Salt Lake City.

In August 1847, the fort was finished. Brigham returned to Winter Quarters to organize his people's trip to their new home.

In 1847, Brigham (in dark coat and hat) and his group of explorers reached the Great Basin.

Chapter Five

Establishing the Promised Land

On December 27, 1847, the Mormons voted for a new president. They had not had one since Joseph Smith was killed. The Mormons elected Brigham as president and prophet. This position gave him an even stronger leadership position in the church.

In May 1848, Brigham led his family and more than 1,200 followers from Winter Quarters to Salt Lake City. One of Brigham's wives, Louisa Beaman Young, gave birth to twin boys on the journey. This group of Mormons arrived in Salt Lake City in the fall of 1848.

Much had changed in Salt Lake City since Brigham had left. The Mormons had built homes and mills. They had dug ditches to bring water to their dry fields. The Mexican War had ended in February 1848, and the Great Basin no longer belonged to Mexico. It was part of the United States.

In 1847, Brigham became the first president of the
Mormon church after Joseph Smith's death.

During the winter of 1848, food supplies ran low. By the spring of 1849, Mormons ate wolves, dogs, crows, and flower roots. Brigham made sure that no one starved. He encouraged the Mormons to share their food or sell it at reasonable prices.

In 1849, many non-Mormons started to use the California Trail. Part of this route followed the Mormon Trail through Salt Lake City. Many of these traveling pioneers were nicknamed 49ers. They had joined the rush to find gold near Sutter's Fort in California.

The 49ers bought thousands of dollars' worth of supplies and services from the Mormons. The money helped the Mormons flourish. But Brigham did not want the Mormons to depend on the money of non-Mormons. They had come to the Great Basin to practice their religion away from outsiders.

The Mormons created their own money system for the proposed State of Deseret.

Mormons and the U.S. Government

Brigham and the U.S. government rarely cooperated with each other. But by leading Mormons to the Great Basin during the Mexican War, Brigham strengthened the U.S. hold there.

Government Relationships

Brigham guided his followers in political matters. He worked with the U.S. government to try to create the State of Deseret. The proposed state included most of present-day Nevada and Utah, plus parts of California, Arizona, Colorado, New Mexico, Wyoming, Idaho, and Oregon.

One problem that blocked the creation of the State of Deseret was whether Deseret should be a slave state or a nonslave state. The Compromise of 1850 was an agreement that solved this problem. The compromise allowed Utah and other western territories to decide whether they would allow slavery.

A second decision was how much territory to allow Deseret to occupy. Part of the Compromise of 1850 gave the Mormons much less territory than they wanted.

Congress did not immediately make Utah a state. Instead, it first created the Utah Territory. Until 1861, it included all of present-day Nevada and part of Colorado. It included part of Wyoming until 1868. The name Utah came from the Yuta, or Ute, Indians who lived there. President Millard Fillmore appointed Brigham the governor of the territory.

A Growing Religion

During the 1850s, the Mormon religion grew. Mormons preached in South Africa, Asia, and Europe. They convinced many people to join the Mormon faith. Thousands of people from all over the world traveled to live in Utah. Most of them followed the Mormon Trail. By 1868, about 62,000 Mormons had taken the trail to Utah. Mormons called this movement of people "The Gathering."

The Mormons built many buildings in Salt Lake City. In 1853, Brigham officially started building the Salt Lake Temple. This building was

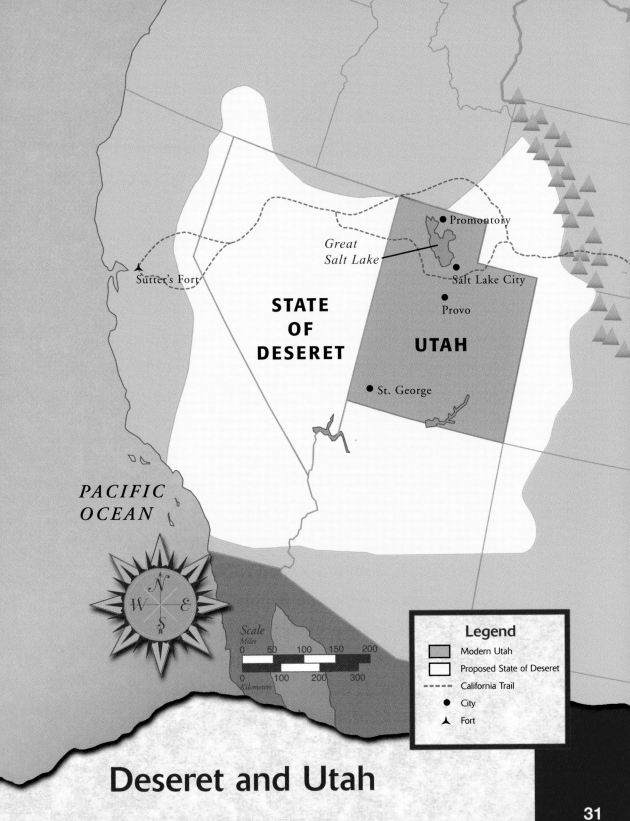

Promontory

Great Salt Lake

Salt Lake City

Provo

UTAH

STATE OF DESERET

St. George

Sutter's Fort

PACIFIC OCEAN

Scale
Miles
0   50   100   150   200

0   100   200   300
Kilometers

Legend

Modern Utah

Proposed State of Deseret

- - - California Trail

● City

⚓ Fort

Deseret and Utah

used for holy ceremonies for church members and their dead ancestors. It was completed in 1893. Brigham built several houses for his large family. His own official home was the Beehive House. His office connected the Beehive House to the Lion House. Most of his family lived in this second building.

At War with the Indians

The Mormons wanted peaceful relations with the American Indians in the Great Basin. The Mormons believed that God considered the Indians to be special people. Mormons wanted to help the Indians learn to farm. But as more Mormons settled on Indian land, the Ute and other Indian nations became angry. During the 1850s and 1860s, the Ute and Mormons fought each other.

In the 1860s, the fighting ended for several reasons. The Ute no longer had enough men to fight the growing Mormon population. Also, Brigham received help from the U.S. Army to fight the Ute. Most of the Ute ended up moving onto reservations. The U.S. government specially set aside this land for them to use, but it was poorer than their original land.

Continued Tension

Over the years, plural marriage continued to anger non-Mormons. Visitors to Utah were shocked to see for themselves that Mormon men had more than one wife. Brigham himself married 27 women and fathered 56 children. The Mormons used the Bible to defend plural marriages. But U.S. laws did not allow the practice. Utah could not become a state as long as plural marriage existed there.

During the late 1800s, Salt Lake City contained a growing population. William H. Jackson created this drawing in 1869.

In 1857, tensions were even higher. President James Buchanan believed that the Mormons were working against the U.S. government. He sent U.S. troops to Utah to make sure the Mormons would be faithful to the country. He appointed a replacement to Brigham as governor.

Brigham and other Mormons feared they would be attacked here as they had been in other places. They organized Mormon fighting units, but before fighting began, the army and the Mormons agreed on a peaceful settlement.

In 1861, the U.S. Civil War (1861–1865) began. Brigham would not allow Mormons to fight for either the Northern or Southern states. Rather than force Mormons to fight, President Abraham Lincoln let them stay out of the war.

Improved Communications

In 1860, the Pony Express improved communications between Utah and the rest of the United States. Pony Express riders carried mail on horseback from St. Joseph in Missouri to San Francisco in California. Riders could deliver the mail in only 10 days. Brigham was impressed that the news from the East could arrive in Utah so quickly.

In late 1861, the first telegraph line connected the East and West Coasts. Brigham understood the telegraph's value for Mormon communication. It carried messages much quicker than the Pony Express did.

Mormons won a contract to build the telegraph line across Utah. They soon organized the Deseret Telegraph Company. Brigham was its president. The Mormons raised money to set up about 1,200 miles

The U.S. government sent troops to Utah to make sure the Mormons were faithful to the United States.

(1,900 kilometers) of telegraph wire in Utah. Telegraph wires soon connected Mormon settlements across Utah.

The Railroad Links East and West

Brigham also understood the value of railroads. In the 1860s, rail companies were building the transcontinental railroad to link North America from east to west. Brigham offered to let Mormon workers prepare the roadbeds for tracks throughout Utah. The rail companies agreed to the arrangement.

In 1869, railroad officials connected the eastern and western railroads near Promontory, Utah. The Mormons used some of their earnings

The railroad linked Utah towns. This photograph shows Salt Lake City about 1860.

from this project to build a railroad linking Salt Lake City to the main track. Railroads soon linked many Utah towns.

An Independent Society

Brigham could see that the railroads were both good and bad for Mormons. He was happy that the railroad would bring new Mormons to Salt Lake City. But he was concerned that non-Mormons and their influences could more easily reach Utah. To avoid those influences, Brigham asked Mormons to join the Zion's Cooperative Mercantile Institution. Mormons were encouraged to shop only with member businesses.

Brigham believed Mormons should be educated apart from the outside world. In 1850, he established the University of Deseret. Today, this school is called the University of Utah. In 1875, he founded Brigham Young University in Provo, Utah. These universities educate young Mormon men and women.

Chapter Six

Remembering a Leader

Health problems troubled Brigham in his old age. At age 69, he developed a painful joint disease called rheumatism. He spent many winters in St. George, Utah. Brigham's rheumatism was less painful in the warm air of this southern Utah town.

On August 23, 1877, Brigham became ill with a mysterious condition. He had cramps, diarrhea, vomiting, and stomach pains. Today, doctors think Brigham probably had peritonitis. This condition occurs when a person's appendix becomes infected and bursts. Brigham was sick for a week.

On August 29, Brigham opened his eyes. He seemed more aware of his surroundings than he had been since his illness began. Brigham looked up and called Joseph Smith's name three times. He then died. Brigham was buried near Temple Square in Salt Lake City.

As an older man, Brigham became ill with rheumatism and other conditions. He died on August 29, 1877.

Brigham spent many winters in a house in St. George, Utah (right). As an older man, Brigham used the hat and cane shown below.

Remembering Brigham

Many Mormons consider Brigham to be an American Moses. Like Moses in the Bible, Brigham led his people to a new land. Today, many people credit Brigham for saving Mormonism after Joseph Smith died. Under Brigham's guidance, the Mormon religion and Salt Lake City grew.

When Brigham died, the newspaper *Deseret News* wrote: "The prophet, having finished his work on earth, had gone into the spirit world to join with Joseph . . . and other great and glorious servants of the Lord, to continue the great work they all labored for on earth."

About 20 years after Brigham died, Mormons officially stopped practicing plural marriage. In 1896, Utah joined the United States as the 45th state.

A photo taken about 1900 shows Brigham's grave in Salt Lake City.

TIMELINE

Chronology of Brigham's Life

Born on June 1 in Whitingham, Vermont

Preaches in England

Marries Miriam Works on October 5

Becomes leader of the Mormons on August 8

- Joins the Mormon church
- Miriam Young dies.

1801	1824	1830	1832	1840–1841	1844

Historical Events

Joseph Smith founds the Mormon religion on April 6.

Joseph and Hyrum Smith are killed on June 27.

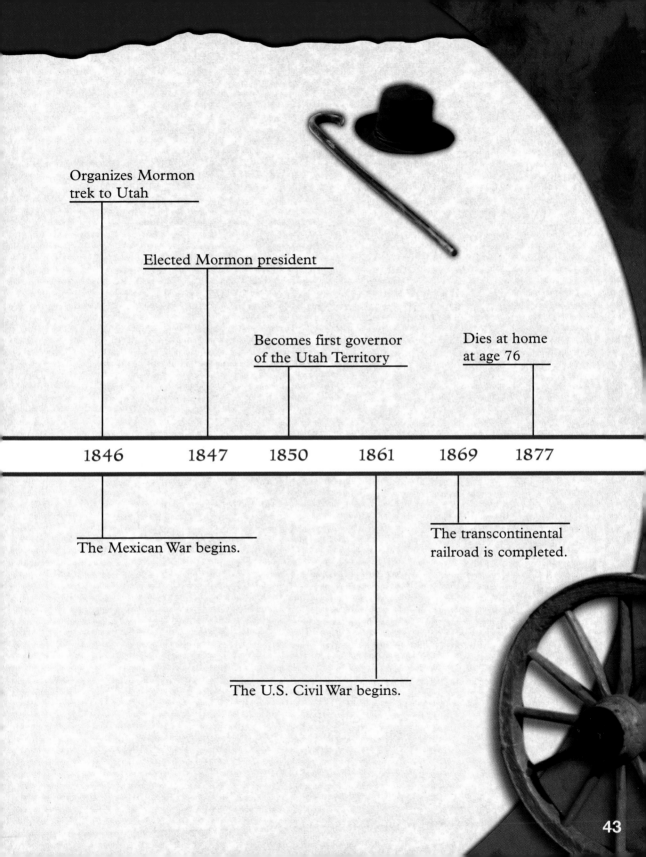

Organizes Mormon
trek to Utah

Elected Mormon president

Becomes first governor
of the Utah Territory

Dies at home
at age 76

| 1846 | 1847 | 1850 | 1861 | 1869 | 1877 |

The Mexican War begins.

The transcontinental
railroad is completed.

The U.S. Civil War begins.

Glossary

49er (FOR-tee NINE-ur)—a person who rushed to find gold in California, starting in late 1848 and early 1849

apostle (uh-POSS-uhl)—one of 12 leaders of the Mormon church

appendix (uh-PEN-dikss)—a bodily organ attached to the large intestine; the appendix can become infected and cause illness or death.

Civil War (SIV-il WOR)—the war between the Northern and Southern United States; the Civil War lasted from 1861 to 1865.

cooperative (koh-OP-ur-uh-tiv)—a business owned or operated by its members.

peritonitis (per-uh-tuh-NYE-tiss)—a condition that occurs when a person's appendix becomes infected and bursts

plural marriage (PLOOR-ul MA-rij)—a Mormon term for having more than one wife at the same time

polygamy (puh-LIG-uh-mee)—the practice of having more than one husband or wife at the same time

Pony Express (POH-nee ek-SPRESS)—a mail service during the early 1860s; Pony Express riders carried mail across the country on horseback.

prophet (PROF-it)—a person who claims to be a messenger of God

trek (TREK)—a slow, difficult journey

tuberculosis (tu-bur-kyuh-LOH-siss)—a deadly disease that affects the lungs and makes breathing difficult

For Further Reading

Blashfield, Jean F. *The Transcontinental Railroad*. We the People. Minneapolis: Compass Point Books, 2002.

Cory Robison, Lynda. *Boys Who Became Prophets.* Revised edition. Salt Lake City: Deseret Book Company, 1998.

Kimball, Violet T. *Stories of Young Pioneers in Their Own Words.* Missoula, Mont.: Mountain Press Publishing Company, 2000.

Kummer, Patricia K. *Utah.* Revised and updated edition. One Nation. Mankato, Minn.: Capstone Press, 2003.

Simon, Charnan. *Brigham Young: Mormon and Pioneer.* Community Builders. New York: Children's Press, 1998.

Places of Interest

Beehive House/Lion House
67 East South Temple
Salt Lake City, UT 84111

The Beehive House was Brigham's official home. Most of his family lived in the Lion House. Brigham's office joined the two buildings.

Brigham Young Cemetery and Mormon Pioneer Memorial Monument
140 East First Avenue
Salt Lake City, UT 84103

The monument contains the grave of Brigham Young and other Mormon pioneers.

Brigham Young Nauvoo Home
Nauvoo Visitors' Center
Main and Young Street
Nauvoo, IL 62354

Brigham lived here in Nauvoo.

Carthage Jail
307 Walnut Street
Carthage, IL 62321

An angry mob killed Joseph and Hyrum Smith at this jail.

Mormon Trail Center at Historic Winter Quarters
3215 State Street
Omaha, NE 68112

Visitors to the museum can learn about the life of Mormon pioneers.

Salt Lake Temple on Temple Square
50 West North Temple
Salt Lake City, UT 84150

The square has landscaped grounds around the Mormon Temple. Brigham preached often at the nearby Tabernacle.

This Is the Place Heritage Park
2601 East Sunnyside Avenue
Salt Lake City, UT 84108-1453

At this spot, Brigham declared that the Mormons would settle in Salt Lake Valley. Copies and originals of buildings from early Utah are on display. Visitors can take tours in covered wagons.

Internet Sites

The Church of Jesus Christ of Latter-day Saints
http://www.lds.org
The Mormons offer official information about their history and religion at this site; a list of places to visit is also available.

Maps of the Mormon Pioneer Trail
http://www.evanstonwy.com/mormontrail/experience/trailmaps.html
Users can view maps of the Mormon Pioneer Trail.

The Mormon Pioneer Trail
http://www.americanwest.com/trails/pages/mormtrl.htm
This Internet site contains the history of the Mormon Trail, including pictures.

Trail of Hope: The Story of the Mormon Trail
http://www.pbs.org/trailofhope
Stories and other information about the Mormon move to the Great Basin are included at this Internet site.

Index

49ers, 28

American Indians, 25, 32
    Ute, 30, 32

Book of Mormon, 14, 16, 24
Buchanan, President James, 34

California gold rush, 28
California Trail, 28
Church of Jesus Christ of Latter-day
    Saints, 4, 5, 14
Compromise of 1850, 29, 30
Council Bluffs, Iowa, 20
Council of Twelve Apostles, 15, 19

Deseret, 24–25, 28, 29–30
Deseret Telegraph Company, 35

Fillmore, President Millard, 30

Gathering, The, 30
Great Basin, 20, 22, 23, 25, 26, 28, 29, 32
Great Salt Lake, 24

Kirtland, Ohio, 14–15, 16

Lincoln, President Abraham, 34

Mexican War, 22, 26, 29
Mormons and westward journey, 6–7,
    20, 22–24, 26
Mormon Trail, 6, 20, 23, 28, 30

Nauvoo, Illinois, 17–18, 19, 20, 21

plural marriage. *See* polygamy
polygamy, 18, 33, 41
Pony Express, 34–35
Promontory, Utah, 36

railroad, 6, 36–37

Salt Lake City, Utah, 6, 24, 25, 26, 28,
    30, 33, 36, 37, 38, 40, 41
Second Great Awakening, 15
Smith, Joseph, 14, 15, 17, 18, 38, 40, 41
    and the *Book of Mormon,* 16
    murder of, 19, 20, 26, 27
St. George, Utah, 38, 40

telegraph, 35–36

U.S. Civil War, 34
Utah, 6, 29, 34, 35, 36, 38
    statehood of, 30, 33, 41
    universities in, 37

Whitingham, Vermont, 8, 9
Winter Quarters, 22–23, 25, 26

Young, Brigham
    baptism as Mormon of, 14
    birth of, 8
    brothers and sisters of, 8, 10
    carpentry shop of, 12, 13
    childhood of, 8
    children of, 12, 33
    death of, 38, 39, 41
    education of, 4, 8
    in England, 18
    health problems of, 38, 39
    jobs of, 10, 11
    and the Methodist religion, 12
    as Mormon president, 26, 27
    as public speaker, 4, 7, 14, 15
    as Utah governor, 30, 34
    wives of, 4, 12, 15, 18, 26, 33
Young, John (father), 8, 10, 11
Young, Nabby Howe (mother), 8, 10, 11

Zion's Cooperative Mercantile
    Institution, 37